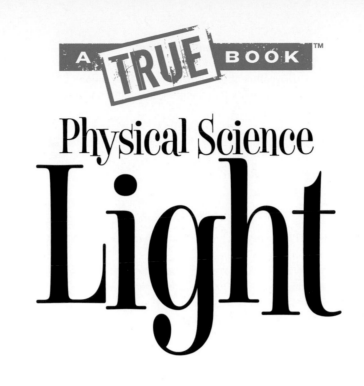

A TRUE BOOK™

Physical Science
Light

JO S. KITTINGER

Children's Press®
An Imprint of Scholastic Inc.

Content Consultant
Valarie Akerson, PhD, Professor of Science Education
Department of Curriculum and Instruction
Indiana University Bloomington, Bloomington, Indiana

Dedication
For Ellie, Ethan, Levi, and James. You are the light of my life!

Library of Congress Cataloging-in-Publication Data
Names: Kittinger, Jo S., author.
Title: Light / by Jo S. Kittinger.
Other titles: True book.
Description: New York, NY : Children's Press, [2019] | Series: A true book | Includes bibliographical references and index.
Identifiers: LCCN 2018034486| ISBN 9780531131404 (library binding) | ISBN 9780531136034 (pbk.)
Subjects: LCSH: Light—Juvenile literature. | Optics—Juvenile literature.
Classification: LCC QC360 .K56275 2019 | DDC 535—dc23
LC record available at https://lccn.loc.gov/2018034486

All rights reserved. Published in 2019 by Children's Press, an imprint of Scholastic Inc.
Printed in North Mankato, MN, USA 113

SCHOLASTIC, CHILDREN'S PRESS, A TRUE BOOK™, and associated logos are trademarks and/or registered trademarks of Scholastic Inc.

Scholastic Inc., 557 Broadway, New York, NY 10012

1 2 3 4 5 6 7 8 9 10 R 28 27 26 25 24 23 22 21 20 19

Front cover: A child outside in the sun
Back cover: Aurora borealis (northern lights)

Find the Truth!

Everything you are about to read is true *except* for one of the sentences on this page.

Which one is **TRUE**?

T or F   People see different colors based on the thickness of a light wave.

T or F   Life on Earth would end without the light and heat from the sun.

Find the answers in this book.

Contents

THE **BIG** TRUTH!

Living Lights

Light can play
tricks with
your eyes.

4

Radio satellite

Physicist Theodore Maiman

Think About It!

Look closely at the photo on these pages. What do you think is going on in the image? What is the girl holding? Why do you think she needs it? What evidence in the photo supports your explanation?

Intrigued?
Want to know more? Turn the page!

Turning On the Light

If you guessed that the girl is trying to see in the dark, you are right! Humans need light to see. During the day, sunlight shines. But at night, it's really dark. Usually, electric lights brighten a building. But what if the lights go out? Light has to come from another source, maybe a candle or a flashlight. Some sources are brighter than others.

The sun, our main source of natural light, is a star.

Tulips need sunlight in order to bloom.

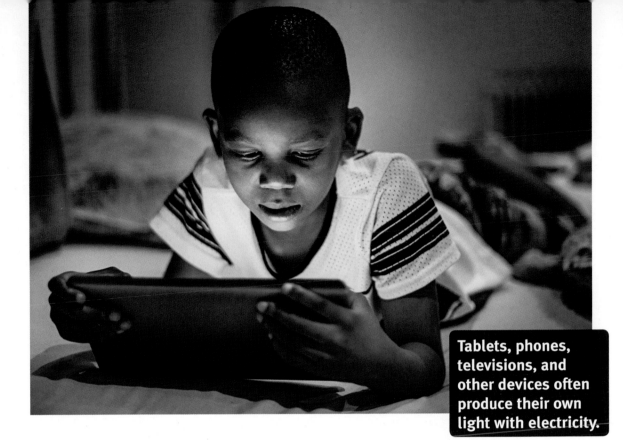

Tablets, phones, televisions, and other devices often produce their own light with electricity.

Most of our light comes from the sun. We also have light when we build a campfire or light candles. Electricity powers the lights in your house. Flashlights and cell phones use electricity stored in batteries. Can you think of other sources of light? Does the moon give us light? No, the moon has no light of its own. It reflects light from the sun.

Humans have used fire for light and heat since prehistoric times.

CHAPTER 1

It's More Than Bright

Light is a form of energy. It comes from tiny particles called atoms. If an atom fills up with energy, it shoots out a small burst of light. Each tiny particle of light is called a **photon**.

The sun is a giant power plant, sending out light and other forms of energy as **electromagnetic waves**. It lets us see and gives us heat. Without light from the sun, Earth would be too dark and cold for life to exist.

The sun, stars, and fire are natural light sources. They create their own light.

Light in Action

The sun is about 93 million miles (150 million kilometers) away, but it is close enough to light the world. Its light shines on the side of Earth facing the sun. As Earth turns, it creates our day and night.

Hundreds of years ago, people generally worked, played, and traveled during the day. The light from candles and oil lamps was weak. But today, bright electric lights allow businesses such as hospitals and factories to operate 24 hours a day.

All our food and the air we breathe depend on sunlight. Do you like fruit? Do cows like to munch grass? Green plants need the sun's energy to live and grow. Some animals rely on these plants for food, and those animals are often food for other animals. But without sunlight, there would be no plants. As a result, we would have no food. In addition, plants give off the oxygen we need to breathe.

Plants use energy from the sun to produce the fruits and vegetables we eat.

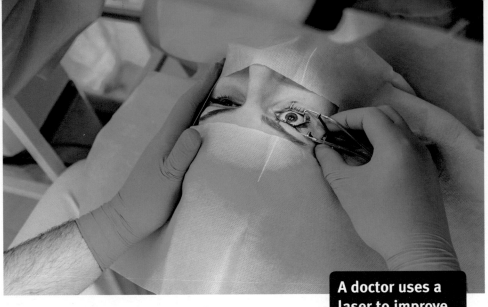

Amazing Lasers

A laser is a human-made light with a narrow beam. Inside the laser device, electricity or another energy source is bounced between two mirrors. The energy source bounces through atoms that produce photons. One mirror is designed to allow some photons through, creating the laser beam. The beam can be red, yellow, green, or blue.

Different lasers cut diamonds, perform surgery, scan bar codes, and do thousands of other jobs. Perhaps you've played with a laser pointer.

Let a Laser Do It

Laser stands for Light Amplification by Stimulated Emission of Radiation. Here are just a few of the tasks lasers can accomplish.

- Read CDs and DVDs
- Clean cavities in teeth
- Cut metal
- Provide a light show
- Help you play laser tag
- Measure speed
- Measure distance
- Reduce acne scars
- Remove tattoos
- Guide a robot
- Scan fingerprints
- Create music
- Guide weapons
- Amuse a cat

A hotel in Singapore puts on a laser light display.

Light takes about 8 minutes
to get from the sun to Earth.

Plants are adapted to
absorb just the right
amount of sunlight.

CHAPTER 2

From Here to There

Light waves travel in straight lines at an incredibly high speed. In fact, nothing travels faster. The speed of light through space is 186,282 miles (299,792 km) per second. If you could fly this fast, you could circle Earth 7.5 times in a second! Light travels 5.88 trillion miles (9.5 trillion km) in a year. That distance is called a light-year.

Light Reactions

When light strikes something, it does one of three things. It reflects, or bounces off. It is absorbed, either partially or totally. Or it passes through something that is **transparent**, such as clear glass.

Drop a ball straight down and it will bounce straight back up. Bounce it at an angle and it will bounce away at an angle. Light bounces the same way.

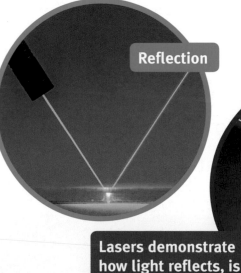

Absorption

Reflection

Passing through

Lasers demonstrate how light reflects, is absorbed by, or passes through materials.

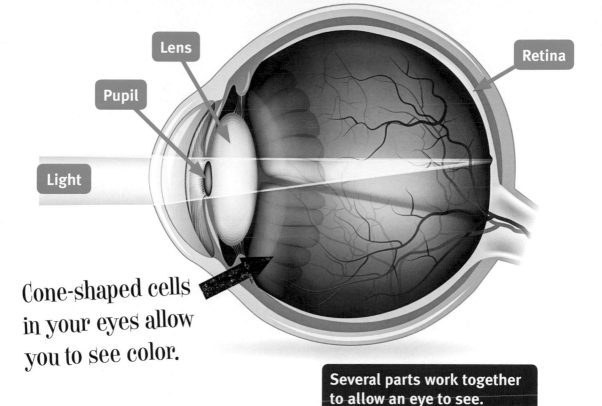

Light

Pupil

Lens

Retina

Cone-shaped cells in your eyes allow you to see color.

Several parts work together to allow an eye to see.

Light in the Eye

When you look at an object, light reflects off the object to your eye. Light enters the eye through the pupil, the black circle at the eye's center, and passes through a clear lens. The lens **refracts**, or bends, the light waves onto the **retina** at the back of the eye. The image on the retina is upside down, but your brain knows to flip it right side up!

The surfaces of most objects have texture. Even a piece of plastic that is smooth to us is rough to a tiny photon. When photons hit these objects, they scatter.

Smooth surfaces, such as a mirror or a very still lake, reflect light waves without scattering them. As a result, the light reflects straight back in the opposite direction. That's why you can see yourself—reversed—in a mirror.

Filling a Room

If light travels in a straight line, how does a lamp light up a room? As light travels through air or water, it hits molecules. These molecules scatter light in all directions the same way a rough surface does. This is called **diffusion**.

Matter can also absorb light. Dark colors absorb light and its heat. Light colors reflect light. That is why you are cooler wearing a white shirt on a hot day.

How many sources of light can you spot in this photo?

Passing Through

Light moves at different speeds through different substances. Water, for example, blocks more light than air does. As a result, light travels more slowly through water. When light passes from air into water, it refracts slightly. In other words, it changes direction. If you fill a glass with water and stick a pencil halfway in, the pencil will look bent. The light hitting the pencil in the water is refracted, and this makes the pencil look refracted, too.

This pencil looks like it's in two pieces due to refraction. It is, however, still in one piece.

It's fun to play with shadow puppets on the wall.

Many materials are **opaque**. Light cannot pass through them at all. For example, light that hits you, a tree, or a building is blocked and makes a shadow. The angle of the light can change the size of a shadow. Try checking your shadow outside at different times of day. As the sun moves through the sky, it shines from different angles. As a result, your shadow can change from a few inches long to several feet taller than you!

From an airplane, a rainbow will appear as a circle.

A special piece of glass called a **prism** also splits light into colors.

CHAPTER 3

In Full Color

Light seems white, but it is full of color! On rainy days, you might see a rainbow in the sky. Sunlight refracts as it passes through the water in the air, splitting the light into seven colors. The colors always appear in the same order: red, orange, yellow, green, blue, indigo, and violet.

Defining Color

Each color has a different **wavelength**. A wavelength is the distance between high points of a wave. Human eyes can see only certain wavelengths. The longest wavelength we see is red. The shortest is violet. All the wavelengths of sunlight together— both those we can see and those we cannot—make up the electromagnetic spectrum.

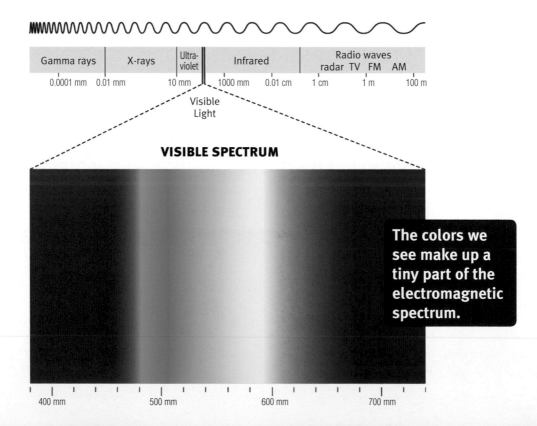

Gamma rays	X-rays	Ultra-violet	Infrared	Radio waves radar TV FM AM

0.0001 mm   0.01 mm   10 mm   1000 mm   0.01 cm   1 cm   1 m   100 m

Visible Light

VISIBLE SPECTRUM

The colors we see make up a tiny part of the electromagnetic spectrum.

400 mm   500 mm   600 mm   700 mm

You need two things to see a rainbow. First, water needs to be falling in front of you. Second, a light source must be shining behind you. The sun and rain can create a rainbow. But you can create one as well! Attach a spray head to the end of a hose. Stand with the sun behind you and spray water into the air. Do you see a rainbow?

Raindrops act as prisms to create a rainbow.

Seeing Color

When light strikes a blue balloon, the balloon absorbs all the wavelengths except blue. The blue wavelengths bounce off and enter your eye. If you see a red ball, only the red wavelengths of light reflect into your eye. Objects have no true color in their matter. Color is seen because the material reflects certain wavelengths. When it's dark, there is no light to reflect, and objects appear simply as black shapes.

Timeline of Light Advances

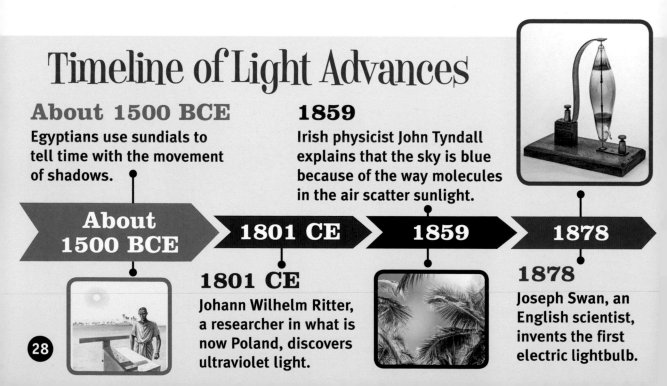

About 1500 BCE
Egyptians use sundials to tell time with the movement of shadows.

1859
Irish physicist John Tyndall explains that the sky is blue because of the way molecules in the air scatter sunlight.

About 1500 BCE | **1801 CE** | **1859** | **1878**

1801 CE
Johann Wilhelm Ritter, a researcher in what is now Poland, discovers ultraviolet light.

1878
Joseph Swan, an English scientist, invents the first electric lightbulb.

Color Blindness

Some people are color-blind. Their eyes cannot see some colors. The most common type affects how people see red and green. Greens might appear more red or yellow, or reds might look greener. Another type affects the colors blue and yellow. It makes blue look greener, or yellow look gray or purple. Total color blindness is rare. Special eyeglasses can help color-blind people see more colors.

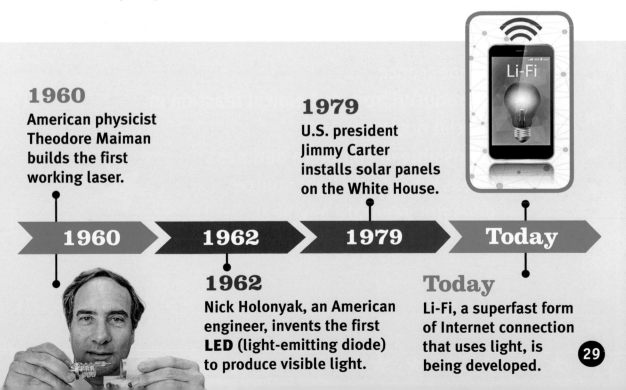

1960
American physicist Theodore Maiman builds the first working laser.

1979
U.S. president Jimmy Carter installs solar panels on the White House.

1960   1962   1979   Today

1962
Nick Holonyak, an American engineer, invents the first **LED** (light-emitting diode) to produce visible light.

Today
Li-Fi, a superfast form of Internet connection that uses light, is being developed.

29

Living Lights

Light from fire or the sun is hot. Some animals, however, can make cool light called **bioluminescence**. Fireflies are the most commonly seen bioluminescent animal. But in the deep ocean, many creatures create their own light. Some of these organisms are trying to attract food or a mate. Others use the light to hide from or scare predators.

How does this light work?

Bioluminescence . . .

- ★ is produced from a chemical reaction in special organs
- ★ is possible in complete darkness
- ★ needs no outside light source
- ★ does not generate any heat

In the air, a firefly can glow for up to 3 seconds at a time.

Huge radio telescopes listen for electromagnetic signals from outer space.

Radio telescopes are the largest type of telescope.

CHAPTER 4

Invisible Light

The colors we see are only a small portion of the electromagnetic spectrum. Beyond them, to both sides of the visible part of the spectrum, is a wealth of invisible types of light. Gamma rays have the shortest waves. Radio waves have the longest wavelength. Other invisible light includes X-rays, ultraviolet rays, infrared light, and microwaves. The shorter the wavelength is, the more energy the wave carries. Look back at page 26 to see a diagram of the full spectrum.

Long Waves

Infrared energy has wavelengths that are too long for us to see, but we can still feel it. Most of it comes from heat! It's in the warmth of the sun and the body heat of a dog. Even you produce infrared energy! It is also how TV remotes change the channel.

Radio waves have even longer wavelengths. They track airplanes in radar systems. They also bring music and weather alerts to the radio.

Short Waves

At the other end of the electromagnetic spectrum are X-rays and ultraviolet (UV) rays. Doctors use X-rays to look at a person's bones, teeth, or other internal body parts. X-rays are painless, but exposure to large amounts is harmful.

Sunlight carries UV rays. Too much UV results in a sunburn. Sunscreen helps protect your skin. But UV rays are not all bad. Your body needs them to make vitamin D, an important nutrient. Police also use UV lights to find evidence.

Ultraviolet light helps an expert look for damages to a painting.

Auroras can be many colors, but green is the most common.

The aurora borealis, also known as the northern lights, shines over the northern reaches of America.

CHAPTER 5

Weird and Wonderful

You may think of light as simply the brightness that comes from the sun or a lamp. But light has some amazing abilities. A thunderstorm brings lightning powerful enough to start fires and topple trees. If you live far enough north or south, you may see the sky blazing with winding, colorful lights. And if you shine UV light on certain minerals, you might be surprised by the way they glow.

Lights in the Sky

Lightning is a discharge of electricity that builds up in a cloud. Most lightning travels within the clouds. But about 100 bolts strike the ground around the world every second.

The aurora borealis, or northern lights, is seen in the sky in the far north. The aurora australis is seen near the South Pole. Auroras are brilliant red or green-blue light displays. They are created when particles from the sun slam into Earth's magnetic field.

Lights From Earth

Certain minerals glow with amazing colors under UV light. The UV light excites electrons in the stone. This releases energy called **fluorescence**. Fluorite, calcite, and dolomite are three common fluorescent minerals.

Our planet doesn't produce its own natural light, but astronauts still see a light display in space. During the day, sunlight reflects off Earth, highlighting oceans and land. At night, electric lights outline our cities and continents. Wherever people go, light energy is there. ★

Different fluorescent minerals produce different colors when they glow.

Bouncing Light

On its own, light travels in a straight line. But can we make it turn corners?

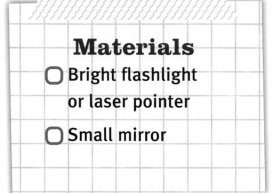

Materials
- ☐ Bright flashlight or laser pointer
- ☐ Small mirror

Directions

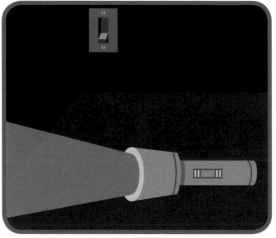

1. In a dim room, turn the flashlight on and lay it on a table or have a friend hold it still.

2. Hold the mirror so the light strikes it. What happens to the beam of light?

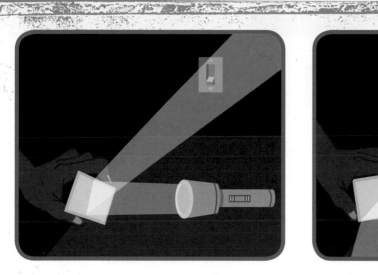

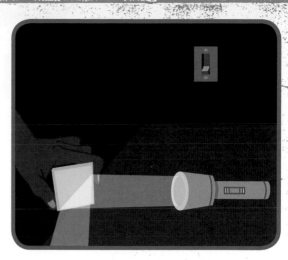

3. Tilt the mirror to change the direction of the light. Try to reflect the light onto the ceiling.

4. Try to reflect the light onto the floor.

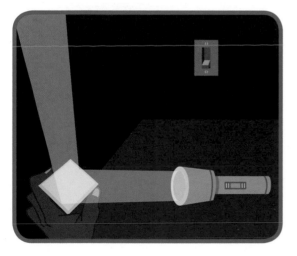

5. See how many other items in the room you can focus the light on.

Explain It!

Using what you've learned in this book, can you explain how you changed the direction of the light beam? If you need help, turn back to pages 20 and 21 for more information.

Waterfall of Light

Mirrors aren't the only items that can bend light. In this activity, we'll create a glowing waterfall!

Materials

- ☐ Small nail
- ☐ Empty 2-liter plastic bottle with a screw top
- ☐ Water
- ☐ Laser pointer

Directions

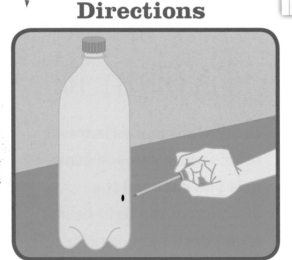

1. With an adult's help, use the nail to poke a small hole in one side of the bottle, about 3 inches from the bottom.

2. Fill the bottle with water and screw on the top. (Water will not flow from the bottle until the top is removed.)

3. Set the bottle on the edge of the sink, with the hole toward the sink.

4. Darken the room. Have a friend shine a laser through the bottle to the bottle's bottom hole.

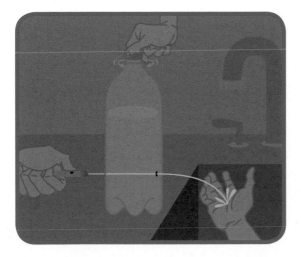

5. Slowly uncap the bottle. Hold your hand under the stream of water flowing from the bottom of the bottle. Does the light appear on your hand?

Explain It!

Using what you've learned in this book, why does the light follow the stream of water? If you need help, turn back to page 22 for more information.

True Statistics

Speed of light in a vacuum, which has no matter: 983,571,057 ft. (299,792,458 m) per second

Distance of one light-year: About 5.88 trillion mi. (9.5 trillion km)

Time it takes for light to travel from the nearest star (not the sun) to Earth: About 4.2 years

Distance from which human eyes can see a candle flame: 1.6 mi. (2.5 km)

Percent of people who sneeze when they look at the sun: Up to 35

Depth that light reaches in the ocean: 656 ft. (200 m)

Most efficient light source: A firefly—100%

Did you find the truth?

F People see different colors based on the thickness of a light wave.

T Life on Earth would end without the light and heat from the sun.

Resources

Books

Kenney, Karen Latchana. *Sound and Light Waves Investigations.* Minneapolis: Lerner Publications, 2018.

Midthun, Joseph, and Samuel Hiti. *Light.* Chicago: World Book, 2012.

Winterberg, Jenna. *Light and Its Effects.* Huntington Beach, CA: Teacher Created Materials, 2016.

Visit this Scholastic website for more information on light:
★ www.factsfornow.scholastic.com
Enter the keyword **Light**

Important Words

bioluminescence (bye-oh-loo-mih-NES-uhns) the ability to produce light as a living organism

diffusion (dih-FYOO-zhun) the process through which particles spread and mix

electromagnetic waves (ih-lek-troh-mag-NET-ik WAYVZ) waves that travel at the speed of light and are made up of electric and magnetic energy

fluorescence (fluh-RES-ens) the light given out by using a certain type of energy, such as ultraviolet light or X-rays

LED (ehl-ee-DEE) a special electrical device that produces light. LED stands for *light-emitting diode*

opaque (oh-PAKE) not clear enough to allow light through

photon (FOH-tahn) a packet of light energy

prism (PRIZ-uhm) a clear, solid glass or plastic shape that breaks up light into the colors of the rainbow

refracts (rih-FRAKTS) changes the direction of a light ray or energy wave from a straight path

retina (RET-uh-nuh) the lining at the back of the eyeball, which is sensitive to light

transparent (trans-PAIR-uhnt) able to let light through so that objects on the other side can be seen clearly

wavelength (WAYV-lengkth) the distance between the high points on a wave of light or sound

Index

Page numbers in **bold** indicate illustrations.

About the Author

Jo S. Kittinger loves science and nature. You will see that passion in many of her books. She is the award-winning author of over 35 books for kids. When she's not writing, you might find her kayaking or photographing the wonders of nature! Jo lives in Alabama but loves to travel and explore the world. Learn more about her at www.jokittinger.com.